My Father For

Children

Praising God Through the Alphabet

An Acrostic Devotional By
Pamela A. Taylor

My Father For Children | Copyright © 2000, 2020 by Pam Taylor

Published by Loaves & Fishes Coaching Inc.
ISBN: 978-1-7351646-4-9

Cover design & book layout by Heather Hart
Cover photography © Wavebreakmedia | DepositPhotos.com
Chapter art © Igors Petrovs | DepositPhotos.com

The author of this book can be contacted for permissions, additional copies, and speaking inquiries at: LoavesandFishesCoaching.com

"Looking forward to that wonderful time we've been expecting, when his glory shall be seen—the glory of our great God and Savior Jesus Christ. He died under God's judgment against our sins so that he could rescue us from constant falling into sin and make us his very own people, with cleansed hearts and real enthusiasm for doing kind things for others."
Titus 2:13-14

With Huge Gratitude...

To my Father God for never giving up on me;
seeking each of us until we find Him.

To Heather Hart for the idea to create a child's edition
of this acrostic devotional book.

Dedicated...

The children who show us how to love in childlike, uncomplicated love.

Thank You.

Introduction

Dear child,

I hope you will write your own prayers or draw a picture of each word of each letter for God. Then share it with your parents, family, or Sunday School teacher. And teach your friends how to use the alphabet to love God and talk to Him all day.

A

My Father, Thank You For Always Being There.

Your Word says…

"…Be sure of this—that I am with you always, even to the end
of the world."
Matthew 28:20b

No matter what happens, no matter how tired I am, or how ill I
feel; no matter how angry or lonely I am, I can run back to the
arms of my loving Father, because You are always there.

Thank You.

B

My Father, Thank You For Believing In Me.

Your Word says...

"Fear not, for I am with you. Do not be dismayed. I am your
God. I will strengthen you; I will help you; I will uphold you
with my victorious right hand."
Isaiah 41:10

Even if I can't believe in myself; even if others put me down or
make fun of me from trying new things; even if it has never
been done before, still, You believe in me.

Thank You.

C

My Father, Thank You For Caring About Me.

Your Word says...

"Give all your worries and cares to God, for he cares about
you."
1 Peter 5:7, NLT

I feel lonely sometimes; everyone is busy, but I can always
count on You, because You care about me.

Thank You.

D

My Father, Thank You For Being Devoted To Me.

Your Word says...

"God has said, 'I will never leave you or let you be alone.'"
Hebrews 13:5, NLV

People move away, friends come and go, and relatives forget they are related to each other, but You are devoted to me.

Thank You.

E

My Father, Thank You For Being Everywhere.

Your Word says...

"The Lord is watching everywhere and keeps his eye on both
the evil and the good."
Proverbs 15:3

In my home, in my play and in my sleep; in the flowers and in
the rain; in happy people and in sad ones. You are everywhere
in my world.

Thank You.

F

My Father, Thank You For Being My Faithful Father.

Your Word says...

"Lord, you are our father! You are the one who has always
saved us!"
Isaiah 63:16b, ESV

Fathers are busy. They have work to do. They travel and
sometimes forget they have families. But I can look to You to be
my forever Faithful Father.

You are too never busy, and You never forget.

Thank You.

G

My Father, Thank You For Being Generous To Me.

Your Word says...

"So I say to you: Ask and it will be given to you; seek and you
will find; knock and the door will be opened to you."
Luke 11:9, NIV

"But if you stay in me and obey my commands, you may ask
any request you like, and it will be granted!"
John 15:7

You love giving me my heart's desires. You tell me to ask and
seek and I will find what I need in You. You are generous to me.

Thank You.

H

My Father, Thank You For Being My Hope-Giver.

Your Word says...

"For I know the plans I have for you," declares the Lord,
"plans to prosper you and not to harm you, plans to give you
hope and a future."
Jeremiah 29:11, NIV

Some of my friends are really confused and sad. I'm glad you
showed me the way. You are my hope-giver.

Thank You.

I

My Father, Thank You For Being Interested In Me.

Your Word says...

> "...when you pray, I will listen"
> Jeremiah 29:12

When it seems no one cares about me or that I am sad. I can stop wherever I am and talk to You, because You are interested in me.

Thank You.

J

My Father, Thank You For Being My Joy-Giver.

Your Word says...

"Then he turned my sorrow into joy! He took away my clothes
of mourning and clothed me with joy."
Psalm 30:11

Whether it is a sad movie or my best friend just moved away,
You fill my emptiness and prove to me that in my sadness, You
are my joy-giver.

Thank You.

K

My Father, Thank You For Your Kindness To Me.

Your Word says...

"Show your amazing kindness and rescue those who depend
on you. Use your great power and protect them from their
enemies."
Psalm 17:7, ERV

Others may ignore or make fun of me, or push in front of me in
line, but I can count on the fact that no matter what -You will
be kind to me.

Thank You.

L

My Father, Thank You For Your Longsuffering.

Your Word says…

"Remember that we are saved because our Lord is patient.
Our dear brother Paul told you the same thing when he wrote
to you with the wisdom that God gave him."
2 Peter 3:15, ICB

Longsuffering means patience in the hard things. You are forgiving, patient, and uncomplaining in all things that we do together, my Father. I am glad to know that You are so longsuffering with me.

Thank You.

M

My Father, Thank You For Your Mindfulness of Me.

Your Word says...

"You have seen me tossing and turning through the night. You have collected all my tears and preserved them in your bottle! You have recorded every one in your book."
Psalm 56:8

Father, You are aware of my pain, disappointments, hurts, and tears. I am never away from Your watchful eye. You are forever mindful of me.

Thank You.

N

My Father, Thank You For Never Being Too Busy For Me.

Your Word says...

> "I know that when I call for help, my enemies will turn and
> run. I know that because God is with me!"
> Psalm 56:9, ERV

Though others may get irritated with my questions, it doesn't matter what time of the day or night that I talk to You. You are never hurried, never too busy.

Thank You.

O

My Father, Thank You For Your Open-Arms.

Your Word says...

"This I declare about the Lord: He alone is my refuge, my
place of safety; he is my God, and I trust him"
Psalm 91:2, NLT

You are wherever I am. You are open-armed, and always a safe.
Your arms are never closed to me – I am Your child.

Thank You.

P

My Father, Thank You For Providing For Me.

Your Word says...

"The Lord is my rock, my protection, my Savior. My God is my rock. I can run to him for safety. He is my shield and my saving strength, my high tower."
Psalm 18:2, ICB

Whatever I need, dear Father, You are it. You are my everything; my provider.

Thank You.

Q

My Father, Thank You For Being Quiet-Spoken.

Your Word says...

"...the Lord passed by, and a great and strong wind tore into
the mountains and broke the rocks in pieces before the Lord,
but the Lord was not in the wind; and after the wind an
earthquake, but the Lord was not in the earthquake; and after
the earthquake a fire, but the Lord was not in the fire; and
after the fire a still small voice."
1 Kings 19:11b-12, NKJV

In this noisy world, where so many people are raising their
voices in order to be heard, You lower Yours. You are quiet-
spoken.

Thank You.

R

My Father, Thank You For Being Right Alongside Me.

Your Word says...

"He lets me rest in the meadow grass and leads me beside the
quiet streams. He gives me new strength. He helps me do
what honors him the most."
Psalm 23:2-3

It is an encouragement to know that I am not alone, Daddy. In
every moment and in all the things I do, You are right alongside
me, holding my hand.

Thank You.

S

My Father, Thank You For Being Steadily Dependable.

Your Word says...

"The Lord is the One who will go before you. He will be with you; He will not leave you or forsake you. Do not be afraid or discouraged."
Deuteronomy 31:8, HCSB

My Father, You are always available and continually, consistently, and steadily dependable, in all things.

Thank You.

T

My Father, Thank You For Being Trustworthy.

Your Word says...

"God is not human, that he should lie, not a human being, that
he should change his mind. Does he speak and then not act?
Does he promise and not fulfill?"
Numbers 23:19, NIV

My Father, it is so good to know that I can believe Your Word -
that You do not lie and You care about me. I am so grateful that
You are trustworthy.

Thank You.

U

My Father, Thank You For Being Unwavering.

Your Word says...

"I have loved you with an everlasting love; therefore, I have
continued to extend faithful love to you."
Jeremiah 31:3b, HCSB

Others don't always show their love, but I know that You are
dependable and unwavering with Your love. I can count on You.

Thank You.

$\mathcal{V}$

My Father, Thank You For Being Victorious.

Your Word says...

"For whatever is born of God overcomes the world. And this is
the victory that has overcome the world—our faith."
1 John 5:8, NKJV

Satan wanted to keep me from You, my Father, but You are
victorious over Satan. Although it looks like he wins
sometimes, I know You win in the end.

Thank You.

W

My Father, Thank You For Wanting Time With Me.

Your Word says...

"The Lord your God in your midst,
The Mighty One, will save;
He will rejoice over you with gladness,
He will quiet you with His love,
He will rejoice over you with singing."
Zephaniah 3:17, NKJV

Sometimes it is hard to remember that You want time with me – and that I don't have to do anything special to earn Your attention. That makes me feel very good, my Father.

Thank You.

X

My Father, Thank You For Being "X"-tatic For Me.

Your Word says...

"And you will seek Me and find Me, when you search for Me
with all your heart."
Jeremiah 29:13, NKJV

That is really awesome, my Father – that You are ecstatic
(super happy) when I seek You and want to spend time with
You. It is hard to understand why someone as important as You
would delight to spend time with me, and yet it is true!

Thank You.

Y

My Father, Thank You For Yearning For Me.

Your Word says…

"Or do you think it's without reason the Scripture says that
the Spirit who lives in us yearns jealously?"
James 4:5, HCSB

The more I spend time in the Bible, reading how You enjoy
Your people, the more I see that You yearn for me; You want to
spend time with me in a personal relationship.

Thank You.

Z

My Father, Thank You For Being Zealous.

Your Word says…

"You will be called the People God Loves, and your land will be called the Bride of God, because the Lord loves you. And your land will belong to him as a bride belongs to her husband. As a young man marries a woman, so your children will marry your land. As a man rejoices over his new wife, so your God will rejoice over you."
Isaiah 62:4b-5, NCV

Earnest, enthusiastic and eager, You are zealous in Your love for me. You shower me with blessings daily. Help me remember You and love You in return.

Thank You.

Got a Minute?

If you enjoyed this book, ask your parents take a moment and let someone know. That way others can know how much fun it is to use the alphabet to know and love God.

Here are a few ways you can show your support:

Write a book review.

Share or mention My Father on social media.
Be sure to use the hashtag #MyFatherAcrosticDevo.

Recommend this book to your friends, family, Bible study sisters and brothers, church family, or anyone else you think might enjoy it as much as you have.

Connect with Pam online by visiting
LoavesandFishesCoaching.com.

About the Author

Pam Taylor is passionately in love with Jesus Christ and delights in walking with Him daily. Her greatest joy has been providing for and raising her two adult children. As a result of being a single, homeschooling mom and former missionary to third world countries, Pam discovered her gifts for teaching, discipling, and writing. She is now a Christian Life Coach and Living Your Strengths Mentor.

You can learn more about Pam and connect with her online at LoavesandFishesCoaching.com

Also Available

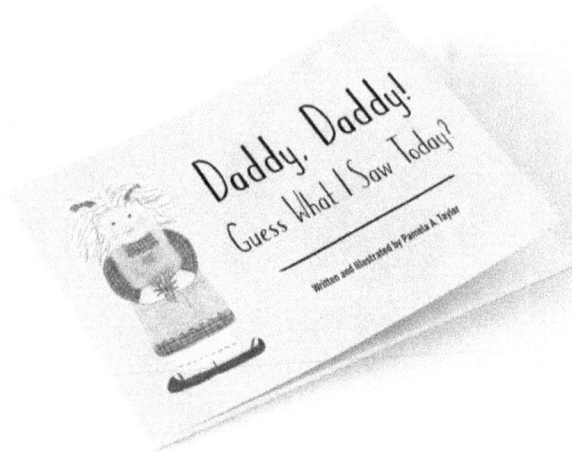

From a flock of geese to a dog on a leash, the pages of this winsome little book are filled with things we see around us every day. Pamela A. Taylor takes those everyday items and looks at them through the eyes of a child; making them seem exciting and new while also teaching children how to be grateful for the God who created them.

Take a walk with Pam through the pages of this book and help your little ones see God's hand in the beauty of life.

Daddy, Daddy! is available wherever books are sold.